To Bill –
Go Bucks!
Blessings,
Kirk Hall

CARSON and HIS SHAKY PAWS GRAMPA

A story about the relationship and love
between a grandfather who has Parkinson's Disease / Essential Tremor
and his seven-year-old grandson

Written by Kirk Hall

Illustrated by Alison Paolini

Publishing

Published by
Innovo Publishing LLC
www.innovopublishing.com
1-888-546-2111

Providing Full-Service Publishing Services for
Christian Authors, Artists, and Organizations: Hardbacks, Paperbacks,
eBooks, Audiobooks, Music, and Videos

CARSON AND HIS SHAKY PAWS GRAMPA

Copyright © 2011 Innovo Publishing LLC
All rights reserved.

No part of this publication may be reproduced, stored in a retrieval system, or transmitted in any form
or by any means electronic, mechanical, photocopying, recording, or otherwise,
without the prior written permission of the copyright holder.

ISBN 13: 978-1-936076-91-8
ISBN 10: 1-936076-91-8

Cover Design & Interior Layout by Innovo Publishing LLC
Cover Art & Illustrations by Alison Paolini

Printed in the United States of America
U.S. Printing History
First Edition: September 2011

IN HONOR OF

The Courage, Determination, and Hope

of fourteen million parents and grandparents worldwide
who live with Parkinson's Disease and/or Essential Tremor

AND DEDICATED TO

The Grandchildren

May they be assured that although our "paws" be weak and shaky,
our love for them remains strong and steady.

Innovo Publishing was pleased to donate its services in the production of this book.
A portion of the proceeds will be donated to help fund PD/ET foundations.

Order *Carson & His Shaky Paws Grampa* or any of our wholesome books online at
www.InnovoPublishing.com.

Hi! My name is Carson, and I am seven years old. I am in first grade, and my favorite class is recess. I live in Colorado with my mom, dad, two sisters, a pain-in-the-neck brother, and a dog named Popcorn. I also have a bunch of aunts, uncles, cousins, and two granmas and grampas. This story is about my Grampa Hall and me.

When I was really little, Granma and Grampa Hall lived in a log cabin with lots of trees and a big fireplace. You could see an awesome mountain called Pikes Peak out the back windows. Sometimes they would have foxes, coyotes, deer, or even a bear go through their yard. It was kind of like an adventure when I was there.

    I don't remember it, but Grampa told me that there were times I would come to stay with them before my brother and sisters were born. He would sit in his favorite chair in front of the fireplace and hold me in his lap. He said he told me lots of stories and sang songs for me. He also said I laughed when he made funny faces and tickled me.

    I remember going to visit when I was older. Granma and Grampa got a dog named Little Fox. He was fun to play with and liked going outside to chase things (but not bears!). He always barks when someone comes in the house, even people he knows—like me. We decided that this was his way of asking, "Who's in my house?"

One time when Granma and Grampa were at my house, Grampa took me for a walk. I was still pretty little, so I sat in my stroller. It was cold and there was snow on the ground. We saw something really funny! Two bunnies were jumping back and forth over each other. They kept doing it for a long time. We still laugh when we remember those silly bunnies.

I remember when Granma and Grampa took me camping for the first time. They have a big tent so there was plenty of room for all of us plus Little Fox. My aunt, uncle, and cousins were there too, and we all went swimming in the stream next to our campsite. It was fun eating at a picnic table by the fire and seeing so many stars!

A couple of years ago, Granma and Grampa moved to a house much closer to where I live. I was sad that I would not be able to visit them at their log cabin any more, but I was very happy that now I would be able to see them more often. I like it when they come over to my house to babysit when my Mom and Dad go somewhere.

After Granma and Grampa moved, I started to notice that Grampa's hands were shaky. And sometimes his head seemed wobbly and he walked kind of slow. My brother and sisters noticed too. I asked him what was wrong. He told us not to worry and that he just had "shaky paws". "Besides," he said, "I can stir my coffee without even trying!"

Grampa and I like watching movies together. At home, we watch DVDs on our big-screen TV. It is nice that we both like the same movies. We also like going to the show to see 3-D IMAX movies like *Polar Express* and eating popcorn. Grampa doesn't drive anymore, so Granma drops us off and picks us up.

Granma and Grampa have taken me skiing a couple times. This year, my Dad (Grampa is his Dad), Grampa, and I went skiing together. We went on some different trails, and I was falling a lot at first, but my Dad helped me while Grampa went further ahead so we could follow him. Grampa and I were pretty tired and slept in the car on the way home.

Grampa's shaking seemed to be getting worse. He got a timer that buzzed to help him remember when it was time to take a pill. I asked him what the pills were for, and he said they were for his shaky paws. Even though he had told me not to worry, I still did once in a while. I think my Dad, Mom, and Granma did, too.

Not too long ago, Grampa told me that he was very excited because his doctor was going to help with his shaky paws. He said he would be going to the hospital three times for a special procedure that would take away his shakiness. He said he looked forward to playing with me without his shaky paws.

Grampa was right! He had the special procedure at the hospital, and now he doesn't shake anymore! He doesn't have to worry about spilling things (like my sisters and brother do). I can see that it is more fun for him now when he plays with me. Mom, Dad, and Grandma are happy. Best of all, I can see that Grampa is happy.

My whole family went to Granma and Grampa's house for Easter. Before we started dinner, Grampa had a prayer he said he wanted to read. I don't remember everything he said, but I think he was giving thanks for his special procedure. He got choked up and couldn't finish. It seemed like he needed a hug, so I gave him one.

So now you know a little bit about my Grampa and me. It didn't matter to me that he had shaky paws. I just like being with him. But I had to come up with another name for him, so now I call him "Old Man" just to tease him. He usually tickles me to get even!

THE END

A NOTE TO PARENTS & GRANDPARENTS

As adults, it is not easy to decide what to tell your children or grandchildren regarding serious illness in the family. Not telling them anything may be a mistake. Children are very intuitive and often pick up on signals that something is wrong. So if we say nothing, they might ask before we have decided what to share, or they may not say anything and imagine the worst. On the other hand, telling them too much can be confusing or frightening. As parents and grandparents, you know your children and grandchildren best and are best equipped to decide what to tell them in these situations. My hope is that reading this book together with your child will provide a natural opportunity for you to broach these subjects.

My approach was to try to keep it as light as possible and to use terminology that my young grandson could understand without causing undue concern. For him, the most obvious symptom of my disease was my shaky hands. So when Carson asked why my hands shook, I just said that I have "shaky paws". He seemed to accept that, at least for the time being.

When the decision was made to proceed with deep brain stimulation (DBS) surgery to eliminate the shakiness, I talked to my son about telling Carson. I decided to share with my grandson that I was excited because the doctors were going to give me a "special procedure" so I wouldn't shake any more. With this information, Carson was aware and knew that I felt good about it.

For now, I think he knows as much as he needs to know. Although DBS is not a cure (there isn't a cure at this time), it should effectively eliminate my shakiness for years to come. By the time Carson is older, other symptoms may become noticeable. At that time, I will share more with him.

Finally, I am open about my faith and how it helps me. By doing this, I am able to share the miraculous gift with which we have all been blessed. Here is the prayer to which I refer in the book and that I wrote for our Easter family dinner:

Thank You for the gifts of hope and blessed assurance that we are reminded of on this day. As I sat with the church choir this morning, it seemed to me that perhaps it was not coincidental that I was feeling "reborn" in a way as I start a new chapter in my life. Thank You for all the blessings You have bestowed on this family. Thank You for the knowledge that we can live life to the fullest, without fear, simply by placing our lives in Your hands.

ABOUT PARKINSON'S / ESSENTIAL TREMOR

It is estimated that as many as six million people have Parkinson's Disease (PD) worldwide and that 50,000-60,000 new cases are diagnosed each year in the U.S. alone. Most people are diagnosed when they are 55 or older, though there are many who are diagnosed at 30 years of age or younger. These people are said to have "early onset" Parkinson's. Parkinson's occurs when the brain stops making a chemical called dopamine, which enables the body to move and helps with your mood. Approximately 10 million Americans have been diagnosed with another movement disorder called Essential Tremor (ET).

Symptoms of PD vary between individuals and may include motor issues such as tremor, stiffness, slowed movement, or balance problems. There also may be a variety of non-motor problems including fatigue, trouble with concentration or memory, cognition, depression, anxiety, motivation, multi-tasking, sleep issues, voice changes, and loss of sense of smell. Essential Tremor is a progressive neurological condition that causes a rhythmic trembling of the hands, head, voice, legs or trunk. It is often confused with Parkinson's disease and dystonia. If you or someone you know is concerned that they may have PD or ET, the most important thing to do is to make an appointment with a movement disorder specialist (MDS), neurologists who are specially trained to diagnose and work with PD, ET, and other movement disorders.

The good news is that there are medications, surgical procedures, and alternative therapies that make living with PD or ET much easier. In my case, the "special procedure" was deep brain stimulation (DBS) surgery, which can be described as a "pacemaker for the brain". Regular exercise has also been proven to be a great way to reduce symptoms. If you have PD or ET, you may want to explore DBS with your movement disorder specialist. It has made a huge difference in the lives of many PD patients.

PARKINSON'S / ESSENTIAL TREMOR RESOURCES

Sources of information for the disease, treatment, support groups, donations, and more:

1. Michael J. Fox Foundation (www.michaeljfox.org)
2. National Parkinson Foundation (www.parkinson.org)
3. Muhammad Ali Parkinson Center Movement Disorder Clinic (http://www.thebarrow.org/Neurological_Services/Muhammad_Ali_Parkinson_Center/index.htm)
4. American Parkinson's Disease Association (http://www.apdaparkinson.org/userND/index.asp)
5. National Young Onset Center (http://www.youngparkinsons.org/)
6. Deep Brain Stimulation information (http://www.medtronic.com/health-consumers/index.htm)
7. International Essential Tremor Foundation (http://www.essentialtremor.org/)
8. Davis Phinney Foundation (www.davisphinneyfoundation.org)
9. Parkinson Association of the Rockies (www.parkinsonrockies.org)
10. European Parkinson's Disease Association (http://www.epda.eu.com/)
11. List of Parkinsons organizations worldwide: (http://www.pdcaregiver.org/Parkinsons_Organizations.html)
12. To get contact information for Parkinson's organizations and support groups in your area go to: http://www.parkinson.org/Search- Pages/Search.aspx?pSearchOpt=Local and http://www.apdaparkinson.org/userND/ChapterLocation.asp
13. For a referral to a movement disorder specialist in your area, contact the Movement Disorder Society in Milwaukee, Wisconsin, at 414-276-2145.

Read more about the *Shaky Paws Grampa* book series and how to support Parkinson's Disease and Essential Tremor research at www.InnovoPublishing.com/Featured-Book-Shaky-Paws-Grampa.html.

ABOUT THE AUTHOR

Kirk Hall lives in Colorado with his wife of 42 years, Linda. Their two sons and their families live nearby. He was diagnosed with ET in 1991 and PD in 2008 and had successful DBS surgery for tremor stemming from both conditions in 2011. Kirk has participated in a variety of clinical research studies at the University of Colorado hospital and the National Institute of Health in Bethesda. Kirk and Linda are active members in the Parkinson's Association of the Rockies. He is also a member of TeamFox. Their active lifestyle includes skiing, camping, hiking, golf, tennis, workouts at the local recreation center, bike riding, babysitting, watching grandkids play sports and more. They are also involved in the life of their church where Kirk is a member of the choir. He recently tried zip-lining in Costa Rica and loved it!

ABOUT THE ILLUSTRATOR

Alison Paolini lives in Northern California where she enjoys a multitude of creative activities. She studied acting and set design in New York and fine art with illustration at California State University at Northridge. She also taught "Drawing On Your Imagination" for eight years at The Paradise Art Center and shows her work at local art galleries. Alison is a published illustrator and poet. She is an active member of the Parkinson's Association of Northern California. She and her husband have two children and three grandchildren. They have enjoyed living in and visiting many parts of the world. Alison was diagnosed with Parkinson's in 1999 and believes firmly that staying creatively active is crucial in coping with the disease.

ABOUT INNOVO PUBLISHING LLC

Innovo Publishing LLC is a full-service Christian publishing company serving the Christian and wholesome markets. Innovo creates, distributes, and markets quality books, eBooks, audiobooks, music, and videos through traditional and innovative publishing models and services. Innovo provides distribution, marketing, and automated order fulfillment through a network of thousands of physical and online wholesalers, retailers, bookstores, music stores, schools, and libraries worldwide. Innovo provides a unique combination of traditional publishing, co-publishing, and independent (self) publishing arrangements that allow authors, artists, and organizations to accomplish their personal, organizational, and philanthropic publishing goals. Visit Innovo Publishing's web site at www.innovopublishing.com or email Innovo at info@innovopublishing.com.

CPSIA information can be obtained
at www.ICGtesting.com
Printed in the USA
263858LV00002B